Persephone
and the
Springtime

The lofty peak of Mount Olympus rises into the blue sky of Greece. There, in ancient days, the deathless gods and goddesses had their home, forever happy. Demeter, the earth mother, was a smiling goddess, but when she came down from Mount Olympus into the valleys, where men lived and worked, she suffered a loss so great that she made the whole earth feel her sorrow. Joy follows sorrow, as surely as the seasons change, and so it happens in this story.

Persephone
and the
Springtime

A GREEK MYTH

Retold by MARGARET HODGES

Illustrated by ARVIS STEWART

LITTLE, BROWN AND COMPANY
BOSTON   TORONTO

Books by Margaret Hodges

THE GORGON'S HEAD

THE FIRE BRINGER

PERSEPHONE AND THE SPRINGTIME

FIRST EDITION

T 04/73

Library of Congress Cataloging in Publication Data

Hodges, Margaret.
   Persephone and the springtime.

   (Myths of the world.)
   SUMMARY: Retells the Greek legend that explains why
Persephone brings springtime to the earth each year.
   [1. Mythology, Greek] I. Stewart, Arvis L., illus.
II. Title.
PZ8.1.H69Pe   292'.2'11   72-7492
ISBN 0-316-36786-9

*Published simultaneously in Canada
by Little, Brown & Company (Canada) Limited*

PRINTED IN THE UNITED STATES OF AMERICA

To the mother I lost
and the mother who took her place

If Winter comes, can Spring be far behind?
— *Percy Bysshe Shelley*

6

Everyone, everywhere, loves the springtime. The ancient Greeks said that spring was a beautiful young girl. Her name was Persephone and she always followed in the footsteps of her mother, Demeter, the earth goddess.

Demeter loved the singing birds, and the poppies blowing in the fields of wheat. She took care of the crops in summer, and in the autumn she gathered in the golden harvest. She watched over her child with tender care. Demeter was happy all year long and in those first days of the world there was no winter. But one terrible year the springtime was lost.

On a sunny day, late in the year, Demeter was in the harvest fields and Persephone wandered off by herself, gathering flowers. She was about to turn back when she saw a strange bush with bright blossoms and a sweet, heavy fragrance.

"How beautiful!" she thought. "I will take it up by the roots and carry it home to plant in my mother's garden."

But this was not easy to do. At last Persephone took hold of the bush and pulled until the earth began to crack and break around the stem. She gave another pull, and thought she heard beneath her feet a sound like the rumbling of an earthquake.

One last pull, and up came the bush, leaving a deep
hole in the ground. As Persephone watched, the hole
grew wider and deepened into a long dark tunnel.

Again came the rumbling noise, nearer and louder. Then four black horses, breathing fire and smoke, galloped out of the earth, pulling behind them a chariot of iron. Holding the reins was a tall man, dressed like a king and wearing a golden crown that flashed with a thousand diamonds. He shaded his eyes as if the sunlight were too bright for him.

Then he seized Persephone and shouted to the four black horses. They turned and plunged again into the earth.

13

Persephone cried out, "Demeter! My mother! Save me!"

But the stranger said, "Do not be frightened. I will not harm you. Zeus, king of all the gods, is my brother. I am Pluto, and I rule a splendid kingdom under the earth. You shall rule there with me and be my queen."

"Take me home!" begged Persephone.

"I am taking you home," answered King Pluto. "My home is a palace of gold. It shall be yours forever."

"I do not want a palace of gold," Persephone sobbed. "Take me to my mother."

Pluto looked displeased. "Foolish girl," he said. "All of my riches will be yours to enjoy. I ask nothing in return except your smile." But Persephone could not smile. She could only weep.

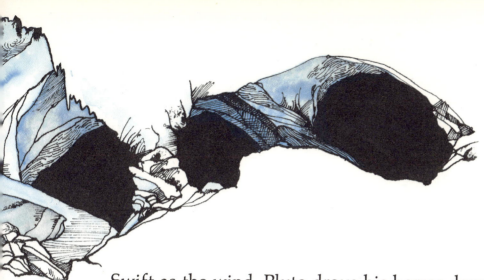

Swift as the wind, Pluto drove his horses downward
and the road grew darker and darker. In the light of
fire that blazed from the horses' mouths and from
sparks struck out by their hooves, Persephone saw rich
veins of gold in the rocky walls around her.

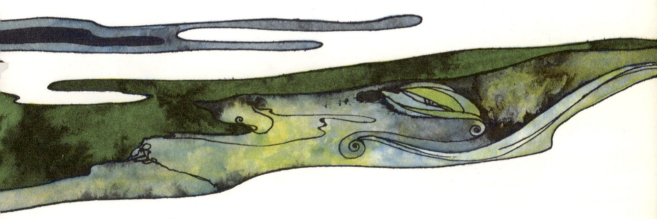

At a tall gateway, Pluto drew rein and great doors
opened. Beyond the gateway flowed a black and slug-
gish stream. "This is the river Lethe," said King Pluto.
"One drink of it and you will forget all sorrow." Then
Persephone heard the sound of barking.

"It is only Cerberus, my watchdog," Pluto said. But this was no ordinary dog. Through the gateway bounded a creature with three ugly heads, each head barking fiercely, and with a tail like an angry dragon, lashing to and fro.

"I am afraid of him!" cried Persephone.

"You need not fear him," said Pluto, "unless you try to run away from me."

He carried Persephone over a bridge and into his palace. Precious stones glowed everywhere like lamps, but there was a gloom over all the dark splendor. Pluto told his servants to prepare a feast and a golden cup of the water of Lethe for Persephone. But she knew well that whoever ate or drank in the kingdom of Pluto could never return home, and so she would not eat or drink.

As for Mother Demeter, when she found that Persephone had disappeared, she set off at once, wrapped in a long dark cloak and carrying a lighted torch of hope and grief, to seek her child.

Day after day, night after night, she searched in vain. She asked the moon goddess to help, but the moon did not know where Persephone was hidden. She asked the wind and the rain, but they could not answer.

At last she asked the sun god, Apollo, who sees all things.

"I know where Persephone is hidden," he said. "I pity her. King Pluto holds her captive in his dread kingdom under the earth."

"Help me," begged Demeter. "Make Pluto let my daughter go free."

"Impossible," Apollo told her. "The sun never goes into that land of shadows."

Demeter was in despair. She no longer cared whether the seeds sprouted or the golden grain ripened. "Let no flowers gladden the earth," she cried. "Let no bird sing. I shall not bless the fields until Persephone comes home."

Then meadows and pastures lay brown and bare. The sheep and cattle starved. The people were hungry. And so six months passed.

Now all this time Persephone had eaten nothing. Like a pale ray of light in the dark cavern of Pluto's palace, she waited patiently. Each day she asked the king to send her home. Each day he looked more sad, more lonely. His servants brought her strange, rich food to tempt her appetite, but all in vain.

At last King Pluto sent his servants to the upper world, hoping to tempt her with fresh fruit. But Demeter no longer tended the fruits, and Pluto's servants found only one pomegranate, shriveled and dry. They brought it to Persephone on a silver dish.

It was the first food from her own sunny world that she had seen for six long months. Hungrily she raised it to her mouth and bit into the pomegranate.

At that moment Pluto came to her with a sorrowful face, saying, "You may go home, Persephone. Zeus, my brother, has commanded me to release you because the people of the earth are starving while I keep you here. You are free. Go to your mother." Then he saw the pomegranate, and he smiled. He knew that Persephone would return to him.

With one backward look at his noble face, Persephone ran all the way home. And as she ran, the path grew green under her feet. Flowers bloomed along the wayside. In the fields the crops sprang up and the cattle began to graze. The farmers found their pastures rich with summer's bounty, and from the fruit trees the birds sang all day long.

Mother Demeter had lost all hope of finding Persephone. The flaming torch in her hand burned low and flickered out. Bowing her head under her dark cloak, she turned toward home.

Then over the brown and barren fields she saw a flash of green, and a well-remembered voice cried, "Mother! Here I am!"

No words can tell how glad Demeter was to see Persephone, but still she was anxious, and asked, "My child, did you eat any food in that land of shadows?"

"Never until this morning," answered Persephone. "But today I bit into a pomegranate and swallowed six of the seeds."

"Alas," said Demeter, "because of those seeds you must spend six months every year in the kingdom of Pluto. And while you are gone, winter will rule the earth, and I shall mourn until you return."

But Persephone comforted her mother. "Do not weep. King Pluto is not unkind. I shall go willingly to be his queen, for he is lonely in that dark palace. He will be glad when I am there. And when the winter is over, the springtime will always come again."

So it is that when you hear the first bird sing, you will know that Persephone is coming across the fields.

292
HO

Hodges, Margaret

Persephone and the springtime

DATE		
APR 5 1984		
OCT 12 1983		
	JAN.31.1990	
OCT 12		
10/10/91 Dempsey		